What!! You're Pregnant Again!! Bite Me!!

by

SANDRA ZACCHINO

authorHOUSE

1663 LIBERTY DRIVE, SUITE 200
BLOOMINGTON, INDIANA 47403
(800) 839-8640
www.authorhouse.com

First published by AuthorHouse 07/12/04

ISBN: 1-4184-1691-6 (e)
ISBN: 1-4184-1690-8 (sc)

Library of Congress Control Number: 2004093441

Printed in the United States of America
Bloomington, Indiana

This book is printed on acid-free paper.

Dedication

This book is dedicated to little Marlena or Daniel who, for whatever reason, was not given the opportunity to be on this earth—yet gave me the strength to realize I still have something to offer to this world and to myself.

Table of Contents

Chapter One
Introduction to My World

Let me just start off by saying if you're reading this book because you're looking for solutions or medical advice on infertility, forget it! I'm writing this book because I'm pissed off and I need to let the world know about it! I'm thirty-something and have been trying to get pregnant for over three years. Now, before you start thinking that three years is not really a long time, let me remind you that many people get pregnant within a couple of months.

I'm not writing this book because my situation is unique, in fact, it is quite common. I'm writing it because rarely does anyone talk about the anger, frustration, bitterness, and loneliness that comes along with infertility.

It's easy to find fertility books on medical procedures and tests—tests that sometimes are inconclusive on why you can't get pregnant.

Don't you just love the *Unexplained Infertility Theory?* It's when you go through a series of painful and intrusive procedures that not only drain you physically, but emotionally as well, just to end up hearing a doctor tell you, "Well, I don't know why you can't get pregnant." I think I'd have to respond, "Gee, I don't know why this stick is shoved so far up your ass!"

I decided to share these emotions with you. I also decided to try and take a more humorous approach because if you are reading this book, chances are you're experiencing infertility and could probably use some laughter.

To tell you a little about myself, I have struggled with my body my entire life. Most of my insecurities and problems stem from my body not appearing, or performing, like the norm. I'm completely athletically challenged. Come on, ladies, some of you can relate to the oh-so-dreaded gym class, especially those who were overweight and athletically challenged. For us, gym was torture.

My whole childhood experience was a nightmare. I was always filled with anxiety because I never felt as though I fit in. I used to daydream about being older and finally secure about who I was. *NOT!*

Why is it that when we're young, we think that somehow as we age our insecurities will magically disappear? Granted, there are a select few that really come into their own as adults, but for the most part, I think our childhood events play a larger role than we can even begin to imagine. I never realized that in my thirties, I'd have days where I'd feel like I'm twelve again. *(And that is on a good day!)* I'm still a very anxious person and, once again, I don't feel like I fit in. The only difference now is that somehow my ass grew bigger but my feet didn't! Although I passed the adolescent nightmare, I'm faced, once again, with my body being the cause of my despair.

I come from a first-generation Italian-American family. That, in itself, is enough to cement a completely screwed-up childhood. Our complete family structure pretty much revolved around food. My fondest memories of my childhood were of good food. I anticipated the end of a school day just to go home and have my afternoon snack; that was my extracurricular activity. It was also what I did best.

3

My parents had fear of the night. Translated, that means you could only get pregnant or do drugs when the sun went down. They overreacted to just about everything. The mere concept of macaroni and cheese could send my father's blood pressure through the roof! And I wonder why I'm in therapy.

My siblings and I always struggled with trying to get them to understand the American way of life. I was never allowed to attend sleepovers at my friends' houses. Just the idea of that sent my mother into a complete state of despair. Little things like that were *always* traumatic in my house. Nothing came easy and there was always a perpetual struggle taking place. I think that's why I'm so accustomed to dealing with controversy and trauma. It became a way of life. My adolescence was a disaster, to say the least.

My weight became even more of an issue. Yes, boys were now the motivation. Let's just say that insecurities and fat knees really put a damper on one's sex life. However, thank God that is over. But the one thing I never thought would be an issue *(even as a child)* was infertility. I figured I deserved that! Although I was a heavy child *(my legs bore a striking resemblance to tree trunks)*, I figured I had the perfect baby-making physique.

Well, nature has a way of kicking us when we're already down. I know that I need to be grateful for what I've got *(we all take for granted certain things)*, but I feel having a baby is a God-given right. It's why we suffer with those damn hormones that make us crave massive quantities of really bad food every month.

The sad thing about infertility is that nobody really thinks about it until it happens to them. Even then, as the months go by (for me anyway), it was a constant state of denial. When I contemplate the time I let slip by, I get a chill down my spine. I feel like this is a nightmare and eventually, I will wake up. Getting my period every month is a constant slap of reality.

As an adult, I've managed to keep my weight in check but not without compromise. When I'm heavy, my breasts are nice and supple. As soon as I lose weight, you guessed it! The first two areas to slenderize are my breasts. So, I have a choice. I can have great breasts, but an ass you can cater your next party on, or I can have a great ass and grace the cover of the next issue of *National Geographic*: *"Tribal Women of Zimbabwe."(You get the picture.)* Once again, nature screwing me. Why must I choose?

Now that you know a little about me and my situation, let's move on to why you're really reading this. I'll tell you why I'm so pissed off and how

I try to cope with the unfairness of nature. As an added bonus, I'll give you some advice on dealing with our private hell. Let's face it—*misery loves company.* I know I don't want to be alone in this situation, and neither do you. So let's move on.

Chapter Two
Your Mate

Ladies, if you're married to the typical guy, as I am, chances are, getting him to talk about the infertility situation is about as easy as convincing Joan Rivers to stay out of the plastic surgeon's office. In other words, getting him to go shoe shopping is probably a more achievable task. I'm not saying that they can't be supportive, but their means of compassion and support pretty much depends on when and where he needs to perform sexually. My husband feels as long as he supplies the sperm, that's all that is required of him. Granted, he did need to get slightly more involved, because he needed to take a sperm test. We should feel oh-so-sorry for our men. They are forced to watch pornography and masturbate until they achieve orgasm in the comfort of their own home. Isn't that tragic? *NOT!* It's a role they've been practicing for their entire lives! My husband managed to fail his first sperm test because he felt he was under too much pressure (quite pathetic). So I basically went through some temporary added emotional trauma because he missed the cup the first time , then used the sperm from the second time around for the test which concluded he was infertile. Oh, thank you hubby! For us, ladies, our tests are not quite so easy or enjoyable.

When you and your mate are watching television and anything regarding pregnancy comes on, did you ever notice the expression on his face? How it immediately changes as he silently prays to the Almighty Lord that you won't ask him to leave it on?

Do you ever get in those moods where you become suicidal as you're reminded of your current desperate situation? My husband can't understand *(like that's a news flash)*, why I could possibly feel the need to torture myself. I'm sure you can relate to this psychotic inner need I speak of. It's when we completely immerse ourselves in self-pity—it's fun!

Let me offer you some words of advice if you really want your mate to *NOT* want to have sex. Just put him on a required baby-making sex schedule. This practically destroys the sexual spontaneity in any relationship. When a man is pressured to have sex, especially when his manhood is being

8

questioned, the experience leaves a lot to be desired. Therefore, the whole idea is not recommended. It's hard to believe that sex could actually feel like a chore. Remember, ladies, this is not based on medical research, just pure hellish personal experiences.

My mate has also been complaining about the expenses involved in our baby-making challenge, and I'm not talking about the medical expenses. Let me put it to you this way, when we started trying to have a baby, I had approximately fifty pairs of shoes and an adequate wardrobe. Now, three years later, I have over four hundred and fifty pairs of shoes, and my wardrobe has tripled. *(You do the math.)* Not to mention that every six months, if I don't get pregnant, I cope by booking a cruise. We've spent a fortune on this infertility situation, and that doesn't even include the medical expenses! Shopping and traveling are my ways of coping with the empty feeling of infertility. Consequently, it makes me feel good when I think about all those women out there with small children who barely get a chance to go to the supermarket let alone go on a cruise. It's my sick, childish way of getting even. *(Yes, there is a lot of anger here!)* Although, after shopping compulsively for over three years, the aftereffect leaves a lot to be desired. It no longer fills the void.

I must also say that after about eighteen months of trying to get pregnant, your mate *WILL STOP* asking if you got your period or not. He knows he is pretty much damned if he does and damned if he doesn't. If he does ask, you feel like ripping his face off. If he doesn't ask, he's a selfish son of a bitch! These emotions are quite normal. Just do what I do, try to get a cruise out of him, or anything else that you've really wanted lately, it just may work.

One day, my husband actually came out and asked me, "Honey, what if, for whatever reason, we can't have a baby?" Before he could even finish the sentence, I think he realized his chances of survival were slim. He never brought that subject up again. I can't understand he feels he can't discuss things with me. *(Wherever did he get such an idea like that?)*

A man gets pretty desperate during these situations. He will do anything to keep you from focusing on the baby-making hell. I do realize he has a very difficult role. I'm not completely insensitive—but fuck him! No matter how hard the situation is for them, it's still nowhere near the torture it is for us. *(I'm sure most of you out there would agree.)* Remember, I'm really pissed off!

And why is it they have to tell me that my husband has over one hundred million sperm, which means every time we have sex, one hundred million little sperm are making their way through my uterus, and you're going to tell me that not one of those little bastards can find their way to an egg? Yet you can slap on your drawers and one pubic hair can make its way through those tiny fibers in your underwear. Yes, this is a bizarre comparison but do you see what I'm saying here?

I guess I do have too much time on my hands. You see, I really do need a child. Why do I have to succumb to society and accept my situation graciously? I just can't. It is completely unfair and there is nothing anyone can say that eases the pain. Unfortunately, not even your mate can make it all go away, although I'm sure if they had that kind of power, they would do all they could *(just to shut you up, that is, and in my case to stop the shopping)*.

12

Chapter Three
Things to Avoid

Ladies, everywhere you turn there are constant reminders of our despair. In order to avoid these, I suggest never leaving the house, never turning on the TV and never opening up a women's magazine. Okay, that's a little drastic *(not so much for me, though)*.

Let's begin with leaving the home. We need food for survival, so the supermarket is inevitable. Words of advice, don't go when you are experiencing PMS. The supermarket is a cornucopia of mothers and their babies. While you are casually shopping, suddenly you are bombarded by mommies making silly noises and gazing into their babies' eyes with such deep love. A moment like this can send you straight from the health food aisle to the junk food aisle. *(You know you won't be leaving that store without some form of chocolate or comfort food.)*

The health club is another place of despair, especially if you attend an all-female gym *(which, unfortunately, I do)*. As you are sweating and getting into your workout, suddenly all the mommies are dropping off, and picking up, their babies from the nursery, discussing their experiences, and complaining about this and that. All you could think about is how much you wish you could be part of the "mommy club," because that's what it feels like. A secret, exclusive club that you can't be a part of because you have not yet experienced the main requirement to be considered a member. *Well, fuck you all!!!* What about our secret club? Women who have babies way too easy really have *NO IDEA* what it's like to experience the perpetual disappointments of not achieving pregnancy. Consequently, I just love those annoying comments from women who have children when you tell them that you're experiencing infertility. My ultimate favorite is, "Are you sure you really want to have kids?" That's enough to make me want to bitch slap the person that says that. *(You're right. I rather enjoyed spending the past three years of my life being in a complete state of despair!)* Don't these women understand what it's like to go to a fertility specialist? Take fertility drugs that make PMS look like a day at the beach? Have a nearly ruined sex life? And experience suicidal tendencies when finding out that someone I know is pregnant? *Why do people say such idiotic things?* And they are blessed with children! Ah, the irony of life!

The mall, yet another realm of torture, especially when walking by the Disney store. Nausea is the only way I can describe that feeling; however, I'm willing to make that sacrifice since the mall is an essential part of my therapy program. I just hold my breath and dive right in. I try to stay focused *(shoes, shoes, and more shoes!!)*. Be sure to avoid Saturdays and Sundays, though, very crucial, unless you are feeling accentually stable *(which doesn't happen for me very often)*. If I'm feeling stable, it usually means I'm in a deep sleep!

Okay, let's move on to television. Avoid LMN. Let me repeat L-M-N. For those of you who don't know what LMN is, it's the *Lifetime Movie Network*—bad news. They advertise that they are television for women. *Yea—women who are emotionally stable and not experiencing infertility.* About ninety percent of the movies are about mothers, children, babies, and pregnancy, and most of them are quite traumatic. Don't do it, take it from me. Then there is the program called *"A Baby Story"* on the Discovery

Health Channel. Don't ever watch this if you are feeling at all vulnerable. You will be crying quite heavily by the end of that program. Unless, of course, you are having a self-pity fest, then I highly recommend it.

As far as women's magazines are concerned, I guess that's quite self-explanatory. Just avoid articles that may instigate your current despair. Stick with magazines that emphasize fashion and exercise, although even these magazines still manage to throw in an article or two about pregnancy or post-pregnancy. Why hasn't anyone created a magazine for baby-making-challenged women? *(I like to use baby-making challenged instead of infertile, it just sounds less clinical and less terminal.)* There are all sorts of magazines out there for pregnant women. It just makes the whole situation worse by emphasizing how normal pregnancy *should be*, and I do stress should be, because those of us that are going through this know that is not the case.

Avoid all baby showers at all costs, unless absolutely necessary. These events can send you straight to the drive-thru of your favorite fast food restaurant, while driving home crying hysterically.

Even insurance companies make you feel inadequate. Any medical testing or procedure regarding infertility is not covered by insurance because it's not routine. *Isn't that a kick in the ass!* I still can't get over that one in-vitro procedure that cost approximately $15,000 and was not guaranteed to work, nor was it covered by insurance. Where the hell does the medical industry come up with that one? Let's just add financially drained into the physically- and emotionally-drained equation.

Needless to say, it is almost impossible to avoid the baby-making hell because in everyday life, we are surrounded by constant reminders. I'm reminded every morning when I open my eyes and I am faced with yet another day of controlling my urges to scream and cry, and wonder, why me. I'm sure this is a question every woman who deals with infertility must ask. As I write this book, several months have passed and still no pregnancy. But, guess what? *We're going on another cruise next month!* More infertility expenses.

I could come up with many more events and activities that tend to remind us of our hell, but I don't feel they are really necessary to mention, considering that practically everything can suddenly set you off into a state of complete depression. The main thing to realize is that how you deal with the emotions is what counts. My personal favorite is to become completely reclusive and eat chocolate frosting *(or coconut—I've found that coconut*

17

frosting is quite good) right out of the can. How you choose to deal with it,

I'm sure, is just fine.

Chapter Four
Family and Friends

Now this is a very difficult topic to discuss simply because your family and friends are the people that love you the most and wouldn't do anything to hurt you or to make you feel bad—right? Then why the hell do they make the most ridiculous comments that really make you question why you discuss this topic with anyone at all! Don't you just love it when they say, "Just relax, and it will happen." Yea, right, relax. The only thing that would allow me to relax in this situation is to be clinically diagnosed as being in a coma. Don't they realize that is the lamest piece of advice? If only it were that simple.

Another favorite is to have a drink. Okay, so becoming an alcoholic is the answer to infertility? That seems to only work for sixteen-year-old-girls who have sex for the first time, not so much for your thirty-something-year-old who has had sex more times than needs mentioning.

Or what about, "Maybe it's not meant to be." Oh yea, right. But that sixteen-year-old, eighty-pound crack whore who was impregnated by a fifty-five-year-old homeless guy was certainly meant to be.

My mother seems to think olive oil is the answer. She thinks I don't eat enough olive oil and that's why I'm not getting pregnant. I know what you're thinking, "What the hell is she talking about it?" As I mentioned previously, my parents were born and raised in Italy. So, really, most of their logic comes from an old-fashioned Italian mindset. In other words, *I really don't know what the hell she's talking about!* Italian expressions translated in English usually don't make a hell of a lot of sense, I've learned that over the years. It's funny, I've spent most of my life trying to avoid the topic of sex with my mother, and she has spent most of her life trying to stop me from having sex. Suddenly, she is calling my spouse and demanding we do it more often. Every time I'm on the phone with her she must interject some kind of comment about my spouse and I "getting busy." I never thought there would be a day when my mother would want me to have sex so badly. Too bad she didn't feel this way ten years ago. As far as my siblings, their situation is completely different. My brother had an instant family, and my sister literally planned her pregnancies. My friends all had normal textbook pregnancies. There is no history of infertility in my family. Here you see how much more frustrating the issue is for me. I feel completely singled out and for what reason, I have no idea. That's what hurts the most, not knowing why I was chosen to go through this. So, going back to my mother's advice, I thought to myself, "Why not?" Eating more olive oil sounds a hell of a lot better than getting dye injected into my fallopian tubes, so I gave it a shot. Well, her advice will never be printed in any medical journals. I'm about ten pounds heavier and although I am browsing the maternity clothes, *it's only to find a shirt big enough to cover my newly-rounded fat ass!*

I don't know how it is for you, but for me, holidays have become horrible reminders that yet another Christmas or another Easter, or any holiday has gone by and still no pregnancy. Not to mention that holidays are when you must face all family members other than your immediate family, and deep down, you know they are thinking, "Why isn't she pregnant yet?" Then you've got your completely insensitive relatives who just come right out and ask you the dreaded question.

You've got the older relatives who just can't understand how a young woman in her thirties has not yet had a child. Back in the olden days, it seems as though infertility was not as commonly discussed, and by the time a woman was thirty she'd already had all her children. I do recommend alcohol on these occasions, just to comfortably numb yourself until it's over. New Year's Eve is especially difficult for me because it's a time to reflect on past events and years gone by. This is not something you should be doing while experiencing infertility. All you want to really do is focus on what is to come in the future.

I realize the topic is difficult for your friends and family because, really, there is not much one can say that is truly comforting. Depending on my mood swings, there are days when I really need to talk about it and yet there are days when I never want to hear another thing about infertility. Apparently your friends and family are not going to exactly be able to predict your mood for any particular day. But your spouse, that's another story. He better know, because he is the one who usually pays the price. All-in-all, even though your friends and family could say some really stupid things, they are truly important in your journey to motherhood. Even though they really don't understand, they are there for you and as lonely as it may

be, having *anyone* willing to listen to you is priceless.

Chapter Five
Don't Really Have a Title

Hey, I have enough on my mind here and then to come up with chapter titles? It has been a little while since the last time I've written anything, not that you would know this. *(I was on my cruise.)* What's funny is that as I was sitting on this luxury ocean liner, sipping Cosmopolitans and socializing with the upper middle class, every so often the thought that I'd rather be home wearing sweat pants and catering to a baby kept eluding me. *(I know that's sick!)* Isn't life so ironic? How many women with children would do anything to go on vacation? Why does human nature have to be so insatiable? What we have is never enough. We always want what we can't have. It's funny, though. I thought the more time that went by, the harder this was going to be for me, but I think I'm becoming comfortably numb.

I even have moments where I question myself. Do I really want kids? Yes, maybe those obnoxious women at the gym may have a point occasionally. It goes back to that old saying, "Be careful what you wish for, you just might get it." And then what?

Recently, I went for my annual pap smear. *(Oh joy!)* I become a complete wreck over these visits, for many reasons. First of all, it just plain sucks! And, I don't know about you, but every time I have to go for my annual visit, no matter how much I try to eat foods that won't cause gas, I get the worst stomach pains right before the speculum is inserted, making the whole ordeal so much more irritating. I then need to concentrate on holding in any gas that may accidentally be released. The whole event is uncomfortable enough. Farting in the doctor's face really pushes the level of humiliation to its limit. And I don't know if I'm alone here, but am I the only person who needs a few cocktails before the visit? You know I was thinking they should have male cocktail waiters in the reception area of the gynecologist's office. By the time you get in there, you are all liquored up. Alcohol is a natural leg spreader. *(Remember that from our teenage years?)* They won't even need the stirrups if they made you wait long enough, and they always do. Heck, you'll be scheduling your next appointment before you're through with your current visit. For me, however, the visits become reminders of another annual exam and no pregnancy. Then the infertility topic will come up, and I must decide what the next step is. What can I handle emotionally? Well, I decided to give my husband another sperm test. I figure he has had enough practice *(minus the cup and the drive to the hospital lab)*. Let's just rule him out completely. So, now we are awaiting the results of that exam. The only highlight to my OBGYN visit was that I weighed less this time. *(Woohoo! Hurray for perpetual stress, it speeds up the metabolism! However, I would not recommend it as the preferred method for weight loss.)*

I guess as far as I'm concerned, I need to get my tubes explored. I actually did the pelvic exam, which by the way emotionally drained me for several months. Thank God the results were good. Deep down, I keep thinking that nothing is physiologically wrong with me, that I will one day know why this wait will be so worth it *(and why my feet are so not proportioned to my ass. It's a shock that I can manage to stand up vertically without tipping over)*.

But I digress, life is such a journey. Granted, taking a shortcut will get you there faster, but the long way around will make getting there so much more worth it. I know, bullshit, enough cliché crap! Waiting sucks! I want to be pregnant *NOW!* I don't think the size of my closet is sufficient for me to be infertile much longer. The wardrobe situation is really getting out of hand. Pregnancy is imminent.

You know, PMS has new meaning, too. And as if nature can be any more cruel, don't you just love the fact that PMS symptoms are almost identical to pregnancy symptoms? Nipples are sore—okay that's good. I feel some cramping in my uterus—that's good. I'm completely erratic—well, that's no different than any other time of the month. I'm even feeling a little nauseous—well, that could be due to the fact that I ate an entire box of cake mix. But combined, these signs could possibly be an indication of pregnancy. So every month you go through those brief moments thinking, "Could this be the month?" And then you pee, and reality strikes a blow again when that lovely shade of pinkish-red appears on your toilet paper and you know, once again, you need to pick yourself up and try again. You wonder, how many more months can you actually handle this? All my husband needs to do is see maxi-pad wrappings in the garbage and he won't even bring up the topic. He knows better. He also knows not to bring up the topic when I start asking him questions like, "Why don't you love me anymore?" and "If your feet are beside each other, how come when you take your socks off they're never both in the same place?" That really sets me off! It really irks me that he can get through this so easily; I don't know if he keeps his emotions well hidden for my sake, or if the reality is that men do have the ability to completely vacate their minds of any thoughts or emotions, which after being married for awhile I do believe is possible.

At first, when I started writing this book, it was a form of therapy for me. I hate to say it, but I really thought that before I'd get very far, I'd be pregnant. *NOT!*

Now, it is quite painful to realize the reality of time gone by. I'm still completely in denial. I refuse to accept the idea that something is wrong with me. I sometimes think the only reason I'm not getting pregnant is because, subconsciously, I don't know if I could really handle it. When a woman gets pregnant quickly she does not have enough time to ponder every little fucking thing. By the time she thinks of everything, she's giving birth, and at that point, it's too late to re-think the situation. When you spend years thinking about every little aspect of having a baby, the fear has too much time to accumulate, especially if you are a completely emotional type of person who feels "I want to control everything in my life," as I am. You know, it just dawned on me that between PMS, the week of my period and now, I've realized the older I've gotten, the more I now experience that damn Wiener schnitzel, I mean mittelschmerz *(the cramping you feel during ovulation)*. What a fucking name for it, just the sound of it gets on my nerves. However, the point is, I have about four to eight days of the month that I actually feel pretty good. But that can fluctuate, depending on how much my husband really gets on my nerves during one of the good days. Then *that* number is reduced. The joy of womanhood.

Chapter Six
P.M. and P.M.

One thing I did neglect to mention is that three years ago, I did get pregnant—and quickly I might add. But about nine weeks into the pregnancy, during a routine sonogram, the doctor discovered there was no heartbeat. Do you want to talk about feeling like your whole life has turned completely upside down? Here I was preparing for motherhood, had quit my job, you know you get into a whole new mind-set, then something like that happens and you have to completely switch gears. It's not easy! The doctor offers me my choices of action. First, I could go home and wait for my body to release the fetus on its own. *(NOT!)* Or I could get the fetus removed while being awake. Or I could go to the hospital and be completely unconscious and have the fetus removed. Well, guess which one I chose? I can't even imagine going home and waiting for excruciating pain and for this fetus to exit my body. What if it happened in the middle of the mall or anywhere else for that matter? Being awake was out of the question. Going to the hospital was my choice. Needless to say this was the worst experience of my life! Now, four years later, I never thought I'd still be without a baby. But okay, here I am, and I must take charge of the situation.

To explain the title of this chapter, ever since that experience, I now refer to all the events in my adult life as pre-miscarriage events and post-miscarriage events, simply because I have yet to feel the same again. I always knew I'd never be someone like Madonna, or a famous anybody, but one thing I always felt pretty confident about in my life was that nothing really bad was ever going to happen to me. Well, after that day, which by the way, during that doctor's visit while I was waiting for my turn, I overheard a phone conversation the doctor was having with one of her patients. When she got off the phone, she confided in me that the woman was having a miscarriage. All I could think was 'Oh God, that poor lady. I can't imagine what she is going through.' Little did I know, I was about forty minutes away from finding out that I did, too. After all of that, I no longer felt secure. I felt completely vulnerable and that we never really have complete control over what happens to us. That is a really scary thought. Leave it to me to bring out the negative. It's what I'm good at.

On a lighter note, I did try and make good from an awful event. I decided to go back to school. I got a degree in accounting. I got braces, colored my hair, and got electrolysis done on my face. I figured if I can't have a baby right now, I'd at least have a chin that you couldn't grate cheese on. I think that's a fair tradeoff, don't you? Now that the novelty of not having to pluck anymore has worn off, I think I'd like to be pregnant now. That's how I've managed to cope with the miscarriage. I figure had I not had the miscarriage, I may have never had the chance to do all those things to improve my life, and that has helped me make peace with it. I do try to value life a little bit more because from personal experience, you may think your life is heading one way, and in a minute, it can completely change. It's funny, though, I look at pictures of myself before and after the dreaded event, and I did look happier and more peaceful before. Now, it is almost like I can tell something is just not quite right. I get really angry when I realize the thirties should be a prime time in a woman's life, and mine are being wasted away feeling inadequate and being quite depressed. I know I have control over how I deal with this situation, and like I mentioned, I try to value the simple things; however, as much as I try, I can't escape my anger. What I also found interesting after my miscarriage was that I never knew until it happened to me how common miscarriages are. Maybe had I known, it would not have been so traumatic. I speak to many women, even women who now have children, and many, at one time or another, have had a miscarriage. It just seems to me there isn't enough information out there about miscarriages and infertility. It is like a topic kept under wraps for one reason or another. I think it needs to be spoken about more, and more information needs to be made available to women on how to cope. However, let's now take a journey through my life during this tumultuous time.

Chapter Seven
Pages from my Journal

Tuesday, June 15, 1999

Today worked 8:00-12:00. I went to the gym. Spoke to Doctor's office, nurse suggested I take a pregnancy test. Well, I did and guess what? I'M PREGNANT!! OH GOD!! I told a few people. My husband brought me flowers and chocolate. We went out to dinner. I can't believe it!!

Monday, June 28, 1999

Today worked 8:00-3:00.After went to gym. I feel so tired. Husband got home late. I feel really angry towards him. I feel so alone in this pregnancy.

Friday, July 2, 1999

Today gym. Worked 1:00-5:00. After, went food shopping. I feel so exhausted. These next eight months can't go fast enough.

Now before I go on, I need to comment on July 2's entry. Here, I was pregnant, and I couldn't wait until it was over. I was too concerned with getting fat. I was too concerned with my own selfish feelings and not focusing on the idea that a human life was growing inside my body *(so I thought at the time)*. Let me just say I really regret feeling the way I did. I sometimes feel like I'm being punished for not appreciating my pregnancy. Okay, enough said. Let's move on.

Tuesday, July 6, 1999

Today did a workout. I feel like this pregnancy is never going to end. I can't wait until February. Tried on my "skinny" jeans and already they are getting tight.

Now isn't that crazy that I was completely absorbed with fitting into my jeans—why? Couldn't I have just enjoyed the beauty of pregnancy? It was moments like that one that I can't help but blame on my childhood. I keep thinking, if only I had had a normal childhood and was not overweight and so obsessed with appearances, would that child have lived?

Sunday, August 1, 1999 (The day before my first sonogram)

I relaxed all day. For some reason I feel really depressed and tired.

Isn't that weird, I had no idea what was really happening to me. I guess somehow I knew something wasn't right.

Monday, August 2, 1999 (Worst day of my life)

Today was absolutely the worst day of my life!! I went to the doctor for a regular visit, not expecting to find out the fetus had no heartbeat. I had a miscarriage (Oh my God!!!) Thank God my husband was there. I freaked out. I feel like this is a nightmare. Didn't sleep at all!!

Trying to sleep after a miscarriage is not easy. Let me just say I never want to go through this again.

Tuesday, August 3, 1999

I think today was even more horrible than yesterday. Checked into hospital. I was a nervous wreck. Thank God I was out during the surgery. Had to wait four hours for the doctor to release me. I was going out of my mind. I'm not bleeding that much or cramping too much, but emotionally I'm a disaster.

Wednesday, August 4, 1999

Today tried to pull myself together. I didn't sleep at all last night. Went into town. It feels good to be out and about. Got home. The people from work sent me flowers. I guess life goes on! Reality really has not set in yet.

Sunday, October 24, 1999

Today we got up early. Left New Paltz, got home around 1:30. I worked out. I'm becoming completely obsessed with this whole pregnancy/birth/labor situation. It is completely wearing me down.

(Little did I know this was just the beginning.)

Saturday, December 25, 1999 (Christmas Day)

Today I worked out. Got ready. Mom and Dad were fighting. Having their annual Christmas argument, don't you just love the holidays? Relatives came over. The day couldn't have gone fast enough. Thought about pregnancy a lot today.

Friday, December 31, 1999 (New Year's Eve)

Today we got up, had breakfast. We did some of the activities around the resort. In the evening got ready, had dinner. Tried not to drink too much. I did my best to stay happy and not cry. Not easy!!

Monday, January 17, 2000

Well, not pregnant! I feel relieved, but disappointed! I am so confused as to what to do. I'm so damn scared, but if I let fear take over, I'll never do it! Oh God, help me!! Had really bad cramps today (added bonus).

Monday, February 14, 2000

Got my period! Oh God, I still don't know what to do about this "baby situation," It's killing me!! Ate a lot today.

Sunday, March 12, 2000

Not pregnant! I have such mixed emotions. Went shopping. I don't know what to do anymore.

Friday, April 7, 2000

Today ran errands. Got cramps. Yep, got my period. Oh God, I never thought even getting pregnant was going to be hard for me. Why Me??? Fought with husband all night.

Saturday, May 6, 2000

Today I'm cramping a bit, but no period yet. Took another pregnancy test, came up negative. I'm scared to death!

Sunday, May 7, 2000

Well, woke up bleeding. I don't know why I was so late this month. God, this is so draining. I don't know what to do!!

Monday, September 18, 2000

Not pregnant! I'm a bit sad. I feel really depressed about life today! Discovered that eating soy nut butter and chocolate frosting combined is quite reminiscent of a Reese's peanut butter cup. Highlight of my day.

Monday, October 16, 2000

Absolutely not pregnant! I'm starting to get concerned!

Sunday, November 12, 2000

Guess what? Not pregnant! Still feel lousy! I can't believe I used a fertility monitor and still nothing. I'm getting really nervous now. Spoke to girlfriend, she is pregnant. I can't help but feel really jealous.

Friday, December 8, 2000

Today woke up with really bad cramps, not pregnant. Cried a lot!! I feel truly defeated.

Wednesday, January 3, 2001

Went to work, not pregnant! I'm taking it a little better this month, I kind of knew. I had no pregnancy symptoms.

Sunday, March 25, 2001

Today sucked!! Got my period. I feel so lost!! I really don't know how to handle this anymore. I just want to escape.

Friday, June 15, 2001

Well, not pregnant! God, I can't take this anymore. I'm really depressed. I am so fucking frustrated. There aren't enough carbohydrates in the world to ease my pain.

Thursday, October 25, 2001

Still nothing! I kind of knew. Very depressed. I can't believe this. Feels like I'm being punished.

Tuesday, December 17, 2001

Today, still nothing. I think I'm getting numb. Booked a cruise for January. Fuck it, if I can't have a baby right now, I need to travel. I'm very depressed, though. I feel so trapped and angry. Nothing comes easy to me.

Friday, February 8, 2002

Today, I'm morbidly depressed. I don't even know how to handle this anymore, whether to cry, scream, freak out, or just accept it. Husband completely unsympathetic. We argued all day.

Thursday, March 7, 2002

Once again it hasn't happened. I scheduled a pelvic sonogram for March 20th. Oh God, I'm already tense and sick to my stomach.

Wednesday, March 20, 2002

Had a very tense morning. Went to hospital, the waiting was brutal. Had sonogram done, everything is FINE!!! Oh God, thank you!!! I'm so relieved I have a healthy uterus. Could you imagine I get pregnant this month?

Thursday, April 4, 2002

Okay, got my period, not pregnant. Do I see a pattern here? So much for a healthy uterus. What the hell is wrong here? I was convinced this was it. It is so much worse when I've convinced myself that this is really it, the reality is so much more harsh and brutal.

Here is a perfect example of my Sicilian heritage. Could I be any more stubborn? Could I possible pick up on the fact I'm not getting pregnant naturally? I don't want to do anything about it. However, I feel the need to complain

Wednesday, May 1, 2002

Got fucking period! I'm so depressed, beyond depressed. Don't know how to feel anymore. I'm so beyond scared. WHY!!!!

Wednesday, July 17, 2002

Yep! Period. The only reason I can cope this time is we are going on our cruise Friday and I can drink myself numb. Although the trauma of wearing a bathing suit in public is not eased by alcohol alone.

Sunday, August 11, 2002

Feeling completely out of control. My days of coping are numbered. Just can't handle this much longer!

Sunday, September 8, 2002

Shall I even mention it! I'm really being tested here!

Friday, October4, 2002

Today got really horrible cramps. Guess what? Shopped all day! Isn't that a shock? I can't stop! I never thought that shopping could create so much guilt, yet satiate a certain emptiness at the same time. I didn't know I could actually find boots in bright pink.

Saturday, November 2, 2002

Today SUCKED!! Got fucking period. Cried most of the day. Don't know what to do. My husband has nothing comforting to say, as usual. Went to bed really early.

Thursday, November 28, 2002 (Thanksgiving Day)

Well, happy Thanksgiving to me. Damn it, got period. Just to make the holidays a bit more "special." Isn't it lovely to sit at the dinner table with brutal cramps trying to get through another holiday with "the family?" And to add to my upcoming holiday season, considering I got my period for Thanksgiving, I will probably get it for Christmas too. Merry Fucking Christmas!!

Wednesday, December 25, 2002 (Christmas Day)

God, if I could only predict other events in my life this way. Got period, was there any doubt? Tried to handle it well. I'm getting used to covering my emotions. Got through the day, no tears, a lot of calories, good for me.

Sunday, January 19, 2003

New Year, new resolutions. Hopefully big changes in my life, and guess what, got my period. New year starting off just peachy. Starting to develop unhealthy relation ship with cats, verging on quite bizarre. Having separation anxiety from them when I leave the house. This is not the behavior of an emotionally stable person. My need to mother is becoming overwhelming.

Sunday, February 16, 2003

Today got period, now there is a news flash. I'm kind of glad I took a lot of pain killers this past month. Year not starting off too well.

I must explain that I had a tooth removed, that is why I was on many pain killers, you could imagine how tragic that was for me, now that you have a little bit of a background on my insane world. Anyway, moving on.

Monday, March 3, 2003

Today we had to take one of our cats to the vet. Turns out we thought he had just a urinary tract infection when in fact, he is in worse shape than we thought. He might need a specialist; he had fluid in his lungs and abdomen. Oh God!

Thursday, March 13, 2003

Today was horrible. Came home found Rocky (my cat) lying on the floor, moaning, rushed him to the vet. Within thirty minutes he was slipping away. We had no choice but to put him down. Turns out he had cancer and we never knew it. I feel like a complete failure. I feel like I neglected him and the poor thing suffered because of it. I cried so much. I feel so empty. I'm truly losing faith in life.

Saturday, March 15, 2003

Instead of getting better, I feel worse. The house is a constant reminder of his absence. I got my fucking period today. And as much as that sucks I'm almost relieved because I sometimes feel I couldn't handle being a mother. Losing my cat made me reevaluate what I think I can handle out of life; this has all been way too much, feel like my world is crumbling.

Sunday, April 13, 2003

Today waited for Mom and Dad to arrive from New York. Got my period as usual, that is about the only reliable thing in my life! Cramps and parents, lovely combination. Well, I guess I won't be telling Mom what she has been so desperately waiting to hear.

Thursday, May 8, 2003

Today, got period! Oh what a surprise. Need a life! Obsessing over cats again. Watched shopping channel all day. That is definitely one of my guilty little pleasures, among other things.

Tuesday, June 3, 2003

Today started out with what I thought would be just another period, but this time I think I might have had another miscarriage. As I was on the bowl, I immediately felt a cold sweat and proceeded to black out, I managed to get myself on the floor, I was in so much pain I couldn't stand it. It literally brought me to tears. Even if I had to go to the emergency room I didn't even know how I'd make it there. Lucky for me we had pain killers in the house. I took one, and within an hour the pain subsided. I fell asleep and when I woke up, I just didn't want to face the fact that I might have just had another miscarriage. Nonetheless, I called my midwife and explained to her the events, dreading the response; she actually told me that due to the time of my cycle, the possibility that it was a miscarriage is highly unlikely. You can imagine the feeling of instant relief at the sound of those words; however, after I got off the phone with her, it dawned on me that the first time I miscarried, it was extremely early in my cycle. Well, let's just say I took her advice, because I liked her thoughts on the matter better than my own. I took a few spoonfuls of soy nut butter and went on with the rest of my day.

June 21, 2003

My Birthday. God do I hate birthdays, especially lately. Just annoying reminders of getting older and failing. It has been approximately four years since I found out I was pregnant the first time. FOUR FUCKING YEARS!!!!! That means four years of emotional hell, four years of compulsive shopping (although my wardrobe is quite impressive. If I was ever a guest on Regis and Kelly, I would not have to worry about what to wear). Four years of avoiding reality. I don't think I want to go on, my credit cards are maxed out and there is no frosting in the house.

July 2, 2003

Got period, what else is new? At least the cramps were tolerable. Been eating a lot of nuts lately, not sure why I'm mentioning this in my journal, but according to Mom, food has a lot to do with getting pregnant, maybe nuts increase fertility. I'm really reaching here, aren't I?

July 28, 2003

Don't you just love the months where it works out that you get your period twice in that one month, isn't that special? I'm sure my husband would rather have his balls ripped off by a pit bull then have me get PMS twice in one month, but don't we love the beauty of nature?

August 23, 2003

It's about 110 degrees outside. I got my period and the air conditioner just broke. Let me just say, my husband left early this morning and I don't think he is coming back for a while. I think the pit bulls are looking better to him by the minute. Even my cats disappeared for the day.

September18, 2003

Feeling a little edgy today. Been having chest pains. Got my period. My doctor wants to put me on Xanax, but as much as I would love to be comfortably numb, unfortunately, I'm still trying to get pregnant.

I need to remain as pure as possible, damn it!! If I only knew when!!!

September 19, 2003

Starting to actually consider taking something for my anxiety. It has become overwhelming. It's not like I need to worry about a pregnancy. Thank goodness the cramps are tolerable this month. Each month is a surprise.

October 13, 2003

So much for purity. Started taking a mild sedative for anxiety. I keep thinking, could you imagine I get pregnant now? Yea right, I think I could be on crack and it wouldn't happen, unless of course, I was a homeless slut. I just keep convincing myself that eventually my anxiety will go away. Didn't accomplish much today. Should be getting period any minute now.

October 14, 2003

Realized mild sedative is making me completely sick. I should have realized that any attempt to relieve my anxiety would be contradicted. I should just stick with what I know best, chocolate and consuming myself in the retail world.

November 1, 2003

We are finally moved into our new home. Been drinking more lately at least I've chosen low-carb beer I don't want to become an unhealthy alcoholic. Don't have a phone hooked up yet, and all I keep thinking is how in the hell can I place an order with the home shopping channel with no links to the outside world? Life is looking grim.

November 11, 2003

We finally have our phone lines hooked up. I've already ordered well over ten pounds of chocolate, you know, just in case of an emergency. I've infiltrated all existing closets in the house.

By the way, this house is over 4000 square feet, just to give you sort of an idea.

I still can't control the shopping urges. You know, life is so ironic here. I have a completely massive wardrobe and I live on 23 acres of land in the middle of the country and I work from home. Wearing leopard pants and stiletto boots to the local country market really isn't all that appropriate.

And I wonder why I haven't made friends all that easily out here.

Still debating whether or not to publish this book. Sometimes I think I should just keep it to myself. Then I think I should share my insanity. It will probably make women feel pretty damn good about themselves.

November 16, 2003

Okay, today will be the last journal entry. I'm sitting here going over all this and I need to wrap it up. Although I have a few more things to say before I go.

Chapter Eight
Running Out of Steam

If you are reading this book, I have to say I'm really shocked. That would mean I actually completed it, published it, and you bought it. I also can't stress enough that as the book is being written, it is getting harder and harder for me to add to it, not because I can't think of anything to write, but because it is actually becoming a painful experience. It reminds me that I have not yet conquered my infertility. It reminds me that so much time has passed and I feel more and more defeated. So many people I know are becoming parents, and have become parents, over the period of time that I'm writing this, and I'm stuck in limbo.

People are starting to ask if I've considered adopting. That scares me. Don't get me wrong, I think people who adopt children are amazing. I have so much respect for them. But for me personally, I can't take that route, not now, anyway. To me, it is like giving up on my quest. I refuse to accept this. It is just not acceptable in my life! I sometimes feel I'm the only one that feels this way, but I know that's not possible. Granted, the possibilities are that if I would just accept this as God's will, I might be coping better. But I'm not there yet. I deserve it, damn it!! How can crack whores and abusive people get blessed with children and I can't? For heaven's sake, if someone like Joey Buttafuoco can be given the opportunity to procreate then so should I. Yes, I may be a little high-strung and may have become quite territorial when chocolate is present in the room, but that shouldn't mean I don't deserve a child. I know, I know. Some of you out there might be thinking, if I'm so fed up, why not do all I can, even if it means going through awful procedures that are not only physically painful but emotionally draining? At least I would be taking action. Ordering the "Today's Special" on the Home Shopping Network is not conducive to pregnancy *(but you can get some great deals that way)*.

Now I have to mention something, and it is completely off the subject. I have become a little too interested in the personal lives of the shopping networks' show hosts. Like, do they have children and are they married, I wonder how they spend their off time. I think this infertility has destroyed the part of my brain that can differentiate what I should be really focused on and what is a complete waste of valuable time. Who fucking cares what these people do! But somehow it interests me.

Can you tell that, as this book progresses, I am regressing. Hell, yes! If I could finish this book without lapsing into an incomprehensible form of speech, I'd say I'm still doing fairly well. You know my real desire to finish this book is merely because it is either get pregnant or finish the book. It has to be at least one, or I think I'd really lose it. Why is it that in order to feel good about life or yourself, some kind of act of greatness needs to be accomplished? It's not enough to just be a good person and to just "ride the wave of life."

I keep wondering if my need for motherhood is just a manifestation of my need to accomplish something creative and meaningful. Motherhood is such a gift of importance and accomplishment, and a lot of women who easily have children don't take the time out to realize what they are given. It really is a gift of nature that is, all too often, taken for granted. Believe me, I know I fall into that category, too, because even though I'm not a mother,

I am a daughter, and I take that for granted, we all do. Unfortunately, when you are denied something, then you really feel the absence.

Oh, by the way I'm looking into our next cruise. You know, if you live in the northeast there are a lot of new cruise lines that are sailing from New York, Virginia, and South Carolina. Just thought that would be a little added useful information, if you like to travel. Fuck it, we don't have kids.

My cat has just sat down directly in front of my computer screen and I can't see a damn thing. Speaking of cats, the other day one of the babies *(I refer to the cats that are under one year old as the babies)* ate something that gave him *HORRIBLE* diarrhea. It was so bad that he couldn't get it all out himself, so he decided to drag his ass all over my rugs. Well, you can imagine the horror when I observed this cat leaving brown stains all over my floors as he passed by. I spent a whole lot of time with paper towels and rug cleaner scrubbing away the mess. Needless to say, I had to wipe his butt numerous times just to help him clean up. Did you ever try holding a cat horizontally, while wiping his ass? Not an easy task. However, you may wonder, what the hell does this disgusting little tale have to do with this book? Well, as I was lying in bed that evening, with the aroma of crap lingering in the air, I thought to myself, what the hell do I want a baby for?

I was completely exhausted from cleaning the mess. What is a baby? A crying, whining, crappy mess that doesn't let you sleep at night. Then they grow up to be ungrateful, whining, money-sucking teenagers that don't let you sleep at night for other reasons. I must be nuts! I was a witch when I was a teenager. I'm surprised my mother still talks to me. I guess that is the beauty of the mother-child bond. No matter what, a mother's love is unconditional. I realize having cats is not quite the same as having children, but the point is: Do I really have the patience, and what is the real basis of my desperate yearning for a baby? I mean, I really, really want a pair of Manolo Blahnik shoes, but does that mean if I get a pair, will I be happy? Will I be through with buying more shoes? Probably not. I realize that many times throughout this book I have strayed off the subject a bit; however, it all links back to the subject in one way or another.

I just recently received an e-mail from a friend of mine who is going to be a father. Don't you just love not hearing from people for months and when they do suddenly contact you, it's to let you know they are going to have a baby? Why is it that people feel this urgency to contact everybody they know (even if they don't speak to you on a regular basis) to tell them they are going to be a parent? On top of that, don't you just love getting those fucking Christmas cards that are basically just a picture of someone's little precious one with a Christmas-themed background? Like, what the hell are you going to do with a picture of a baby you have absolutely no relationship with? You will probably never meet the child, and you haven't spoken with the parents in years. I understand practicing this between family and close friends, but last year, I actually received pictures of children whom I never even met! I just had a need to vent a little, forgive me. I haven't had my chocolate therapy for the day yet.

By the way, another year has gone by and I'm still not pregnant— just keeping you updated. The other day, I was invited to a baby shower. Yea, okay, that is exactly the way I want to spend my Saturday. Do you think the subject of pregnancy will come up? Baby showers for infertile women are like the ultimate act of cruelty. We not only have to seem happy for the bitch that's having the baby, but we have to buy her a damn gift, too. Not to mention the misery of being surrounded by women who feel the need to describe every little fucking grueling detail of their own pregnancy and birth experiences, as they proceed to give their useless thoughts and advice on why I may not be getting pregnant. Shall I go on? Am I going to the party? I'm still thinking about it.

Another Mother's Day has come and gone. That day is especially difficult. I keep thinking that my child would have been over three years old by now. As much as I've gotten over that, I'll never forget, nor will I ever stop asking: Why was that a gift I was not allowed to keep?

My birthday is next weekend. We are going on four years since I was pregnant the first time. *FOUR FUCKING YEARS!!!* Even as I say it, I can't believe it. I just can't get myself to accept it. I know, I'm stubborn; however, I keep wondering at what point I wjill make a choice to do something. When it's too late?

My husband is thirteen years older than I am. I really don't want to be wiping the drool off his chin during our child's graduation from school. I'd like him to be lucid. I'm not asking for much, you know. At this point, I think I even convinced myself that one child would do it for me. One child and five cats. That could work. Well, now six again. My husband has a tendency to bring home everything he finds on the road–animals that is. He brings them home and I have to take care of them *(just like a man)*. Why can't he find a sexy male European dancer on the side of the road and bring him home? I wouldn't mind taking care of that!

Well, hello again. It has been several months since I've written. I go through these many phases. Sometimes I can handle it, and sometimes I just can't. One thing is for sure–I'm still not pregnant. It has been quite ironic, lately. I have come across some reading material written by women who had the same idea as I did–writing of their personal infertility experiences and trying to make it humorous. The one difference is that they all succumbed and took some kind of grueling action in order to get pregnant. Some do, some don't. I refuse to torture myself in every possible way in order to get there. You can call it being too passive, or too scared. Nonetheless, I can't bring myself to go through it. I realize I may be only hurting myself, but that's what I do best. I *really* am my own worst enemy.

So much has happened over the months. I've experienced a full-blown nervous breakdown, I've realized the older I get, the less I am able to deal with stress. I think I've officially become a crazy cat lady, and last, but certainly not least, I realized how versatile ground turkey is. Is this what happens to women who don't have children? Or is it just me?

We are now moving into a bigger house and I've been quite preoccupied with packing my closet. It has taken a lot out of me. It's amazing how long it takes to pack four hundred and fifty pair of shoes. All

I can really think about though, is how much more of a pleasant experience this would be if I was either pregnant or had a child. It just seems almost useless to go through life without the joy of a child. A bigger home and a good life in every other aspect, except for one huge empty void that I've come to realize no material object can fill. My chest pains have increased and gotten more intense. I'm wondering at this point if I would even be a fit mother. Then I think, hell, yes! If Courtney Love can be a mother, so can I. Doesn't that just kill you when you think of the most unfit role models that are blessed with children? The thought of alcohol and drugs seems more and more appealing because at least if you don't get pregnant, the hallucinations will fill the void.

My days are numbered. We are soon moving out and I won't have the luxury of being able to concentrate, so I need to bring this book to a close soon. I can't quite figure out how to bring this sordid story to an end. I'm even torn about that decision. I also don't know what I'm having for dinner tonight. Forgive me, but I've lapsed into writing down my inner monologue, Okay, I'm back. Anyway, as I was saying, I really could just go on and on with this book because like I've mentioned before, it has been my only outlet considering everyone else in my life is sick and tired of hearing about it. But I do realize there is only so much I could say without

repetition, and that being said, here are some final thoughts.

Chapter Nine
Okay, Some Other Thoughts First

I keep thinking of more things to say. I've told a few people I was writing this book, and I've had some really good reactions. Most people ask, "Well, what if you get pregnant? Will you finish writing the book? Will you let the readers know?" My thought on that is, if I get pregnant while writing this book, fuck the readers. I'm pregnant!!! No, I'm kidding. I'd finish the book, and I'd let the readers know the outcome because I know that I would be interested in knowing. Not to mention it just might give women out there some hope. And if I don't get pregnant, it will let women out there know they are not alone. So far, the way this is going, I can say that I don't think I'm there yet. I still think that it will happen. I don't know when, but it will.

This has been a very slow and somewhat painful process simply because, most of the time, I really try not to think about it all. But when I'm sitting here in front of my computer, I'm forced to emerse myself in the emotions I've endured. I know you're wondering why I am forced to sit here and write about this when no one really cares whether I write this or not. But I figure, if people had empathy for Suzanne Somers, who published a book about her crash after the sitcom *Three's Company...(Call me strange, mind you, I have not read the book. But having your husband get you fired from a highly rated sitcom simply because of his pompous attitude, to me, is not quite all that worthy of compassion.)* Poor thing was left with a ton of money and highly recognizable stardom,although she now sells great shoes , boots and yummy sugarfree chocolate on HSN got to love her for that, But once again, I digress. I think this book needs to be published. I'm not only doing this for me, but for all the women out there who feel the same way I do, but just didn't know how to express themselves and expose how they really feel.

I've learned some valuable lessons through this journey. I realized it's very hard to concentrate on writing with the *Home Shopping Network* on in the background. I've learned that when your cat sits directly in front of your computer screen, it's time for a break; and that I have so much more respect for writers now that I realize the time and concentration involved in writing a book. This is like a pamphlet compared to the novels out there, yet it has taken a lot out of me.

I realized I can't draw to save my life, but did you get a load of that drawing on the cover? I figured if I was going to be raw and real about my emotions, I may as well let it all hang out. It really takes a passion, or a strong conviction about something, to be motivated to complete a book. Let me tell you, I am motivated.

There seems to be so very little out there that we can control, but I'll be damned if I let my emotions take over and stop me from saying everything I feel I need to get out. I'm at the point now when I can no longer comfortably discuss the topic of infertility with my friends or family. This book is my only outlet. I realize I may have been quite redundant throughout, but there are certain things I can't get past.

Chapter Ten
Final Words

Well, now we know our mates aren't going to make it all go away. Society does nothing but remind us of what we have not yet achieved. Television can be torture, and our friends really don't have anything encouraging to say. So, ladies, it's up to us to cope on our own. It's amazing how common infertility is. Yet, when you're experiencing it yourself, the loneliness is unbearable. You can be in a room full of hundreds of people, but the reality is you feel completely alone. We must realize we are not alone and that we need to approach the situation in our own individual ways, and that no one way is better than the other.

I also promised that I would let you know my current situation by the end of this book. Here it is.

SANDRA ZACCHINO

Tuesday November 11, 2003

Well, woke up with really bad cramps. You guessed it; need I say more?

About The Author

Sandra Zacchino is a Native New Yorker who now lives in central Virginia. This is her first book and was primarily motivated to help women who have suffered through the pain and frustration of miscarriage and infertility without realizing how common and often woman experience these issues. She has taken a humorous approach in order to bring some levity to a more than serious subject. She not only exposes very openly her deepest emotions but she also poked fun at herself in how she deals with her own despair. This book is not intented to solve or provide medical advise, however it offers laughter to women who may feel they are in a very lonely place.

www.ingramcontent.com/pod-product-compliance
Lightning Source LLC
Chambersburg PA
CBHW020347290526
45785CB00005B/2182